Impressum
Verlag: BABADADA GmbH, Nedderfeld 112 , 22529 Hamburg
Geschäftsführer / Verlagsleitung: Harald Hof
Druck: Books on Demand GmbH, In de Tarpen 42, 22848 Norderstedt

Imprint
Publisher: BABADADA GmbH, Nedderfeld 112 , 22529 Hamburg, Germany
Managing Director / Publishing direction: Harald Hof
Print: Books on Demand GmbH, In de Tarpen 42, 22848 Norderstedt

Schule

school

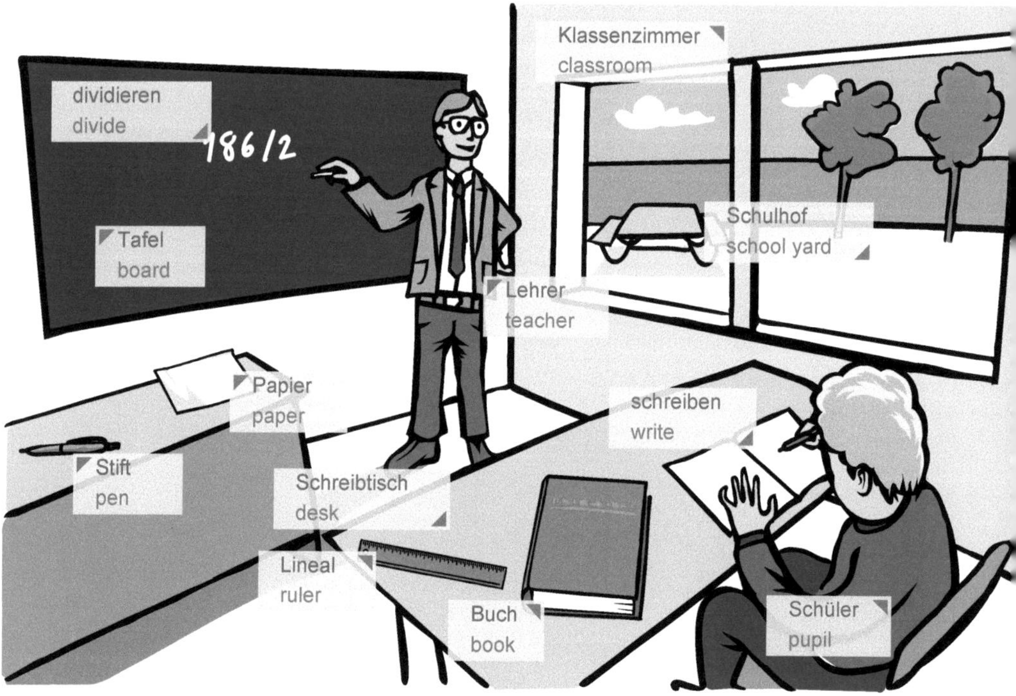
Klassenzimmer
classroom
dividieren
divide
186/2
Tafel
board
Schulhof
school yard
Lehrer
teacher
Papier
paper
schreiben
write
Stift
pen
Schreibtisch
desk
Lineal
ruler
Buch
book
Schüler
pupil

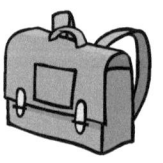

Schultasche

satchel

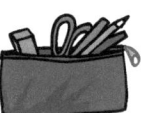

Federmappe

pencil case

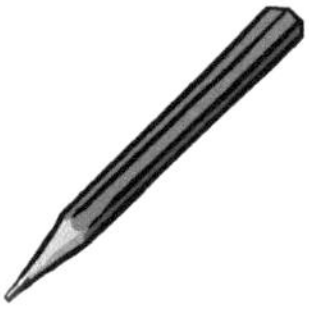

Bleistift

pencil

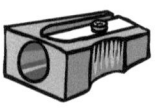

Bleistiftspitzer

pencil sharpener

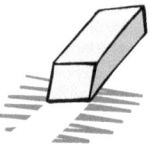

Radierer

rubber

Zeichenblock

drawing pad

Zeichnung
drawing

Pinsel
paintbrush

Malkasten
paint box

Schere
scissors

Klebstoff
glue

Übungsheft
exercise book

Hausübung
homework

12

Zahl
number

2+2

addieren
add

5-2

subtrahieren
subtract

2×2

multiplizieren
multiply

rechnen
calculate

A

Buchstabe
letter

ABCDEFG
HIJKLMN
OPQRSTU
VWXYZ

Alphabet
alphabet

hello

Wort
word

Text
....
text

lesen
....
read

Kreide
....
chalk

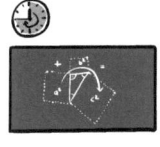

Unterrichtsstunde
....
lesson

Klassenbuch
....
register

Prüfung
....
examination

Zeugnis
....
certificate

Schuluniform
....
school uniform

Ausbildung
....
education

Lexikon
....
encyclopedia

Universität
....
university

Mikroskop
....
microscope

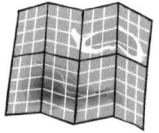

Karte
....
map

Papierkorb
....
waste-paper basket

Reise
travel

Hotel
hotel
Grand
Herberge
hostel
ROOMS
EXCHANGE
Wechselstube
currency exchange office
Koffer
suitcase
Auto
car

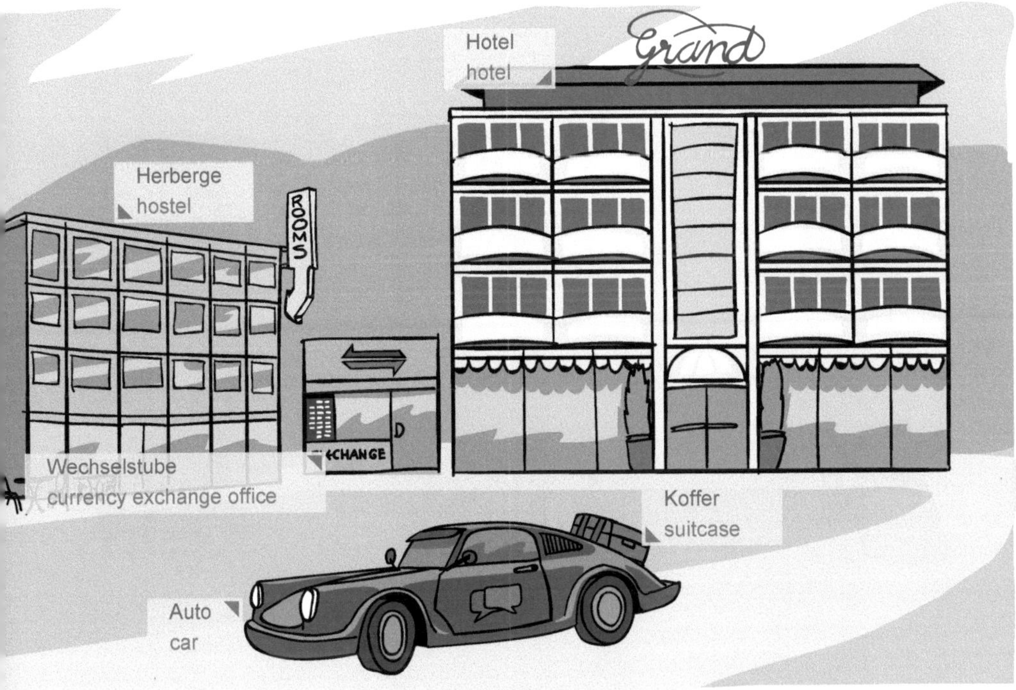

Sprache
language

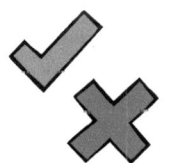

ja / nein
yes / no

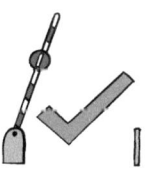

Okay
Okay

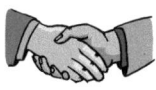

Hallo
hello

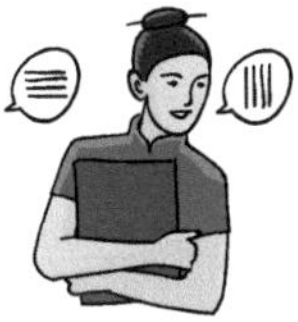

Dolmetscherin
translator

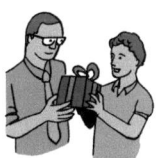

Danke
Thank you

Wie viel kostet …?

how much is…?

Ich verstehe nicht.

I don´t get it

Problem

problem

Guten Abend!

Good evening!

Guten Morgen!

Good morning!

Gute Nacht!

Good night!

Auf Wiederschaun!

goodbye

Richtung

direction

Gepäck

luggage

Tasche

bag

Rucksack

backpack

Gast

guest

Zimmer

room

Schlafsack

sleeping bag

Zelt

tent

Touristeninformation

tourist information

Strand

beach

Kreditkarte

credit card

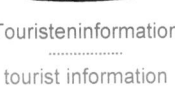

Frühstück

breakfast

Mittagessen

lunch

Abendessen

dinner

Fahrkarte

Ticket

Lift

elevator

Briefmarke

stamp

Grenze

border

Zoll

customs

Botschaft

embassy

Visum

visa

Pass

passport

Transport
transport

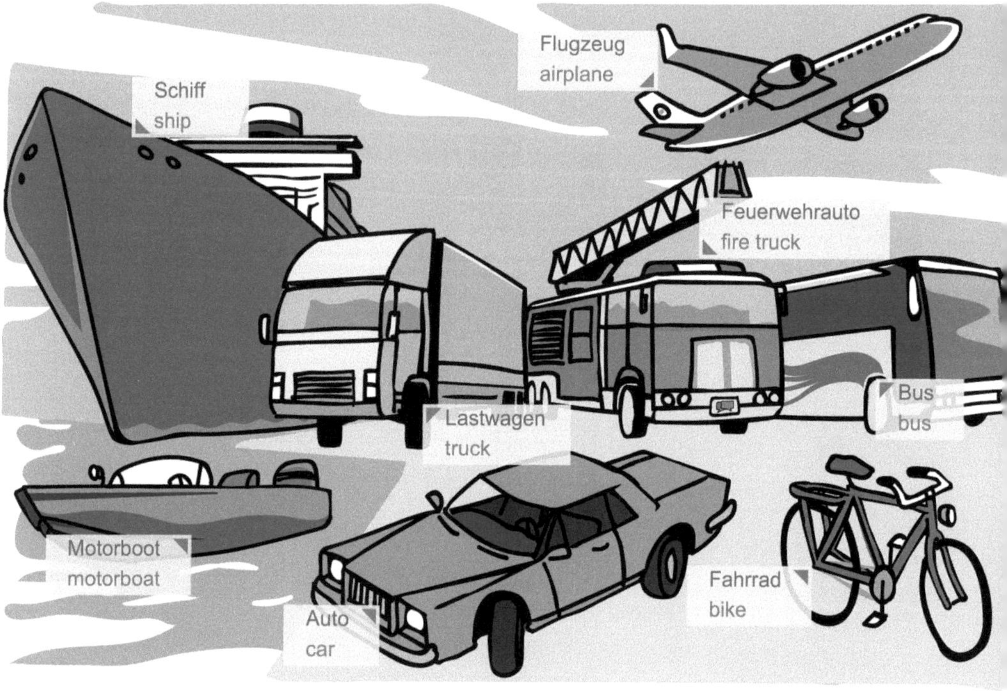

Flugzeug
airplane
Schiff
ship
Feuerwehrauto
fire truck
Bus
bus
Lastwagen
truck
Motorboot
motorboat
Fahrrad
bike
Auto
car

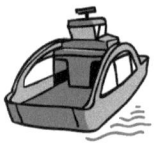

Fähre

ferry

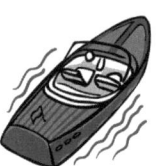

Boot

boat

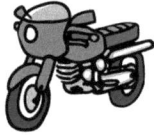

Motorrad

motorbike

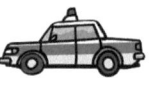

Polizeiauto

police car

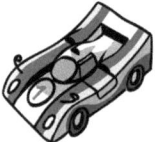

Rennauto

racing car

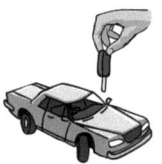

Mietwagen

rental car

Carsharing
car sharing

Abschleppwagen
tow truck

Müllwagen
garbage truck

Motor
engine

Kraftstoff
fuel

Tankstelle
fuel station

Verkehrsschild
traffic sign

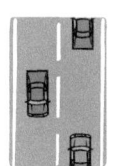

Verkehr
traffic

Stau
traffic jam

Parkplatz
parking lot

Bahnhof
train station

Schienen
tracks

Zug
train

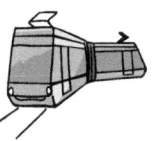

Straßenbahn
tram

Wagon
wagon

Hubschrauber

helicopter

Flughafen

airport

Tower

tower

Passagier

passenger

Container

container

Karton

carton

Rollwagen

cart

Korb

basket

starten / landen

take off / land

Stadt
city

Dorf

village

Stadtzentrum

city center

Haus

house

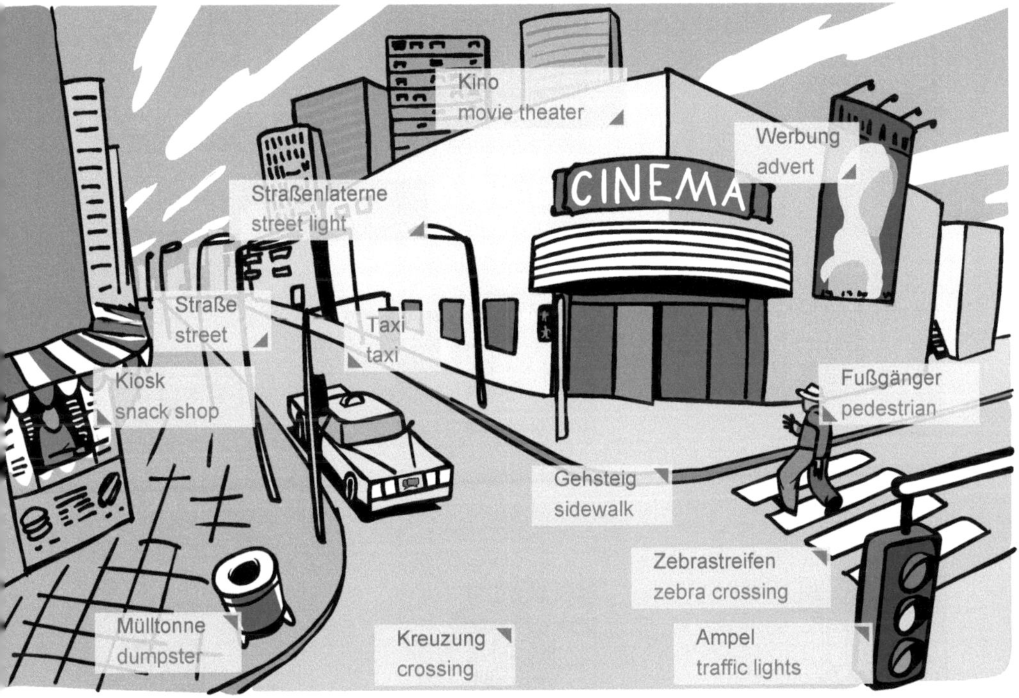

Kino
movie theater

Werbung
advert

Straßenlaterne
street light

CINEMA

Straße
street

Taxi
taxi

Kiosk
snack shop

Fußgänger
pedestrian

Gehsteig
sidewalk

Zebrastreifen
zebra crossing

Mülltonne
dumpster

Kreuzung
crossing

Ampel
traffic lights

Hütte

hut

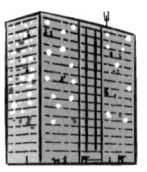

Wohnung

apartment

Bahnhof

train station

Rathaus

city hall

Museum

museum

Schule

school

Stadt - city

11

Universität
university

Bank
bank

Spital
hospital

Hotel
hotel

Apotheke
pharmacy

Büro
office

Buchhandlung
book shop

Geschäft
shop

Blumenladen
flower shop

Supermarkt
supermarket

Markt
market

Kaufhaus
department store

Fischhändler
fishmonger's shop

Einkaufszentrum
mall

Hafen
harbor

Park

park

Bank

bench

Brücke

bridge

Stiege

stairs

U-Bahn

subway

Tunnel

tunnel

Bushaltestelle

bus stop

Bar

bar

Restaurant

restaurant

Briefkasten

postbox

Straßenschild

street sign

Parkuhr

parking meter

Zoo

zoo

Badeanstalt

swimming pool

Moschee

mosque

Bauernhof

farm

Umweltverschmutzung

pollution

Friedhof

cemetery

Kirche

church

Spielplatz

playground

Tempel

temple

Landschaft
landscape

Blatt
leaf

Wegweiser
signpost

Weg
path

Wiese
meadow

Stein
stone

Wanderer
hiker

Baum
tree

Fluss
river

Gras
grass

Blume
flower

Tal

valley

Hügel

hill

See

lake

Wald

forest

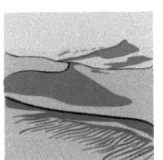

Wüste

desert

Vulkan

volcano

Schloss

castle

Regenbogen

rainbow

Pilz

mushroom

Palme

palm tree

Moskito

mosquito

Fliege

fly

Ameise

ant

Biene

bee

Spinne

spider

Käfer

beetle

Frosch

frog

Eichhörnchen

squirrel

Igel

hedgehog

Hase

hare

Eule

owl

Vogel

bird

Schwan

swan

Wildschwein

boar

Hirsch

deer

Elch

moose

Staudamm

dam

Windrad

wind turbine

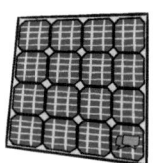

Solarmodul

solar panel

Klima

climate

Restaurant
restaurant

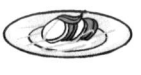

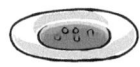

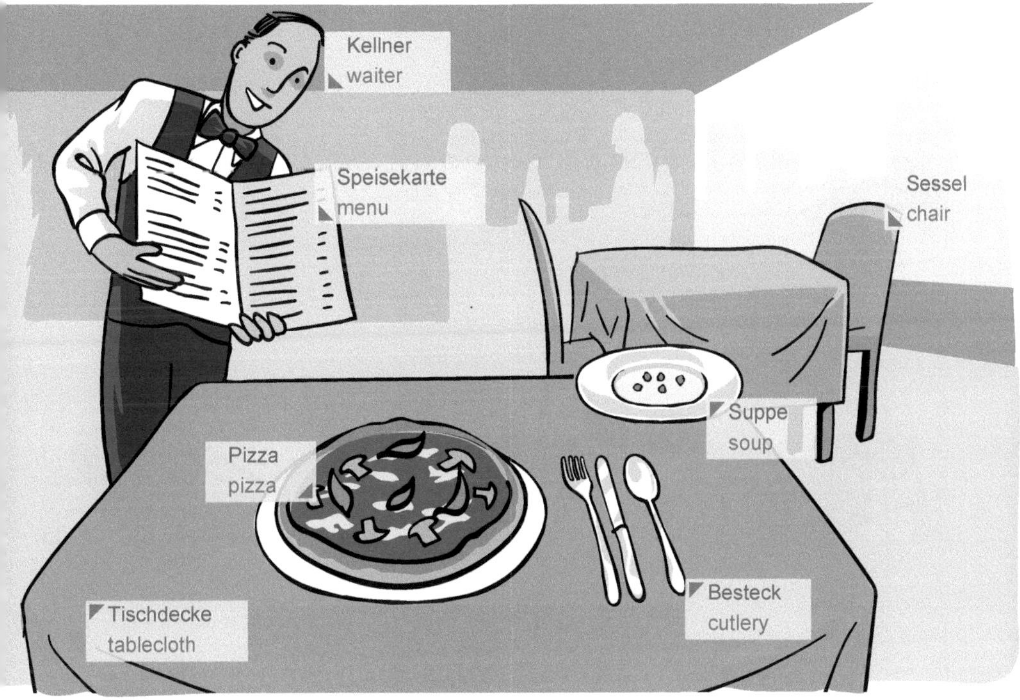
Kellner
waiter
Speisekarte
menu
Sessel
chair
Suppe
soup
Pizza
pizza
Besteck
cutlery
Tischdecke
tablecloth

Vorspeise

starter

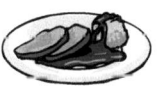

Hauptgericht

main course

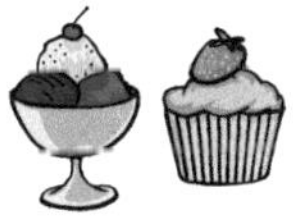

Nachspeise

dessert

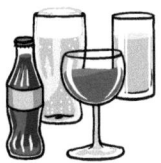

Getränke

drinks

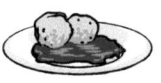

Essen

food

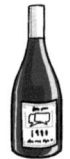

Flasche

bottle

Fastfood

fast food

Streetfood

street food

Teekanne

teapot

Zuckerdose

sugar bowl

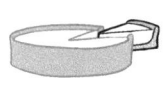

Portion

portion

Espressomaschine

espresso machine

Kinderstuhl

high chair

Rechnung

bill

Tablett

tray

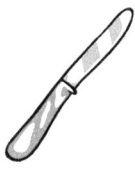

Messer

knife

Gabel

fork

Löffel

spoon

Teelöffel

teaspoon

Serviette

serviette

Glas

glass

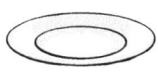		
Teller	Suppenteller	Untertasse
plate	soup plate	saucer

Sauce	Salzstreuer	Pfeffermühle
sauce	salt shaker	pepper mill

Essig	Öl	Gewürze
vinegar	oil	spices

Ketchup	Senf	Mayonnaise
ketchup	mustard	mayonnaise

Supermarkt
supermarket

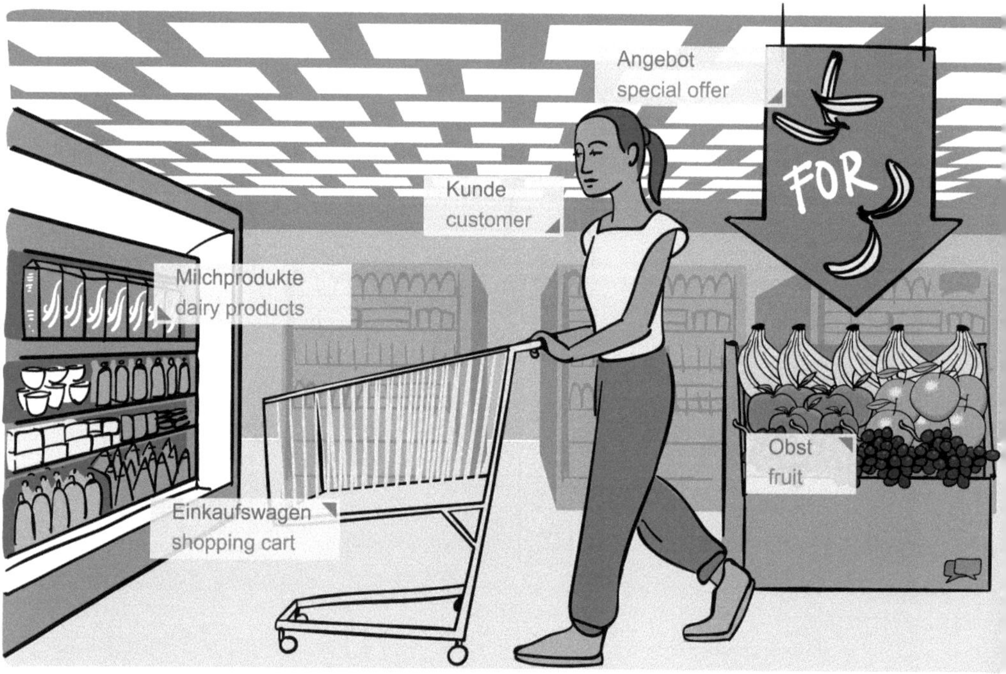

Angebot
special offer
FOR
Kunde
customer
Milchprodukte
dairy products
Obst
fruit
Einkaufswagen
shopping cart

BUTCHERS

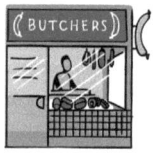

Schlachterei

butcher's shop

BAKERY

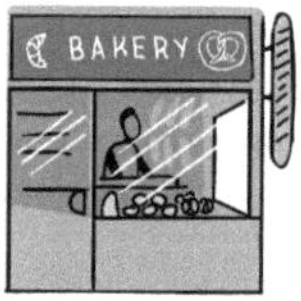

Bäckerei

bakery

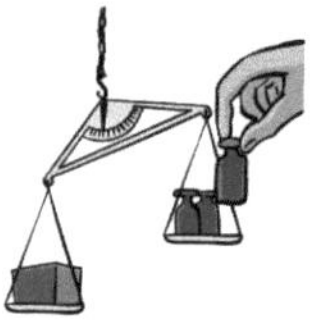

wiegen

weigh

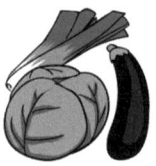

Gemüse

vegetables

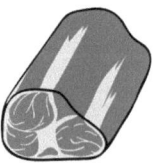

Fleisch

meat

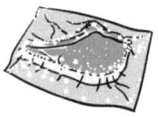

Tiefkühlkost

frozen food

Aufschnitt

cold cuts

Konserven

canned food

Waschmittel

detergent

Süßigkeiten

candy

Haushaltsartikel

household products

Reinigungsmittel

cleaning products

Verkäuferin

sales representative

Kassa

cash register

Kassiererin

cashier

Einkaufsliste

shopping list

Öffnungszeiten

opening hours

Brieftasche

wallet

Kreditkarte

credit card

Tasche

bag

Plastiktüte

plastic bag

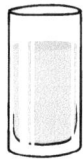

Wasser

water

Saft

juice

Milch

milk

Cola

coke

Wein

wine

Bier

beer

Alkohol

alcohol

Kakao

cocoa

Tee

tea

Kaffee

coffee

Espresso

espresso

Cappuccino

cappuccino

Banane

banana

Apfel

apple

Orange

orange

Melone

melon

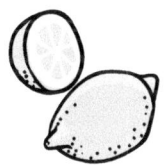

Zitrone

lemon

Karotte

carrot

Knoblauch

garlic

Bambus

bamboo

Zwiebel

onion

Pilz

mushroom

Nüsse

nuts

Nudeln

noodles

Spaghetti

spaghetti

Reis

rice

Salat

salad

Pommes frites

fries

Bratkartoffeln

fried potatoes

Pizza

pizza

Hamburger

hamburger

Sandwich

sandwich

Schnitzel

escalope

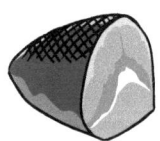

Schinken

ham

Salami

salami

Wurst

sausage

Huhn

chicken

Braten

roast

Fisch

fish

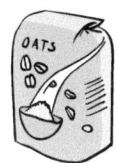

Haferflocken

porridge oats

Müsli

muesli

Cornflakes

cornflakes

Mehl

flour

Croissant

croissant

Semmel

bread roll

Brot

bread

Toast

toast

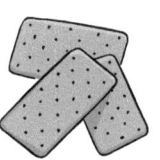

Kekse

cookies

Butter

butter

Topfen

curd

Kuchen

cake

Ei

egg

Spiegelei

fried egg

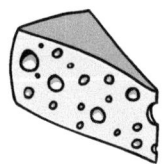

Käse

cheese

Eiscreme

ice cream

Zucker

sugar

Honig

honey

Marmelade

jelly

Schokoladenaufstrich

nougat cream

Curry

curry

Bauernhof
farm

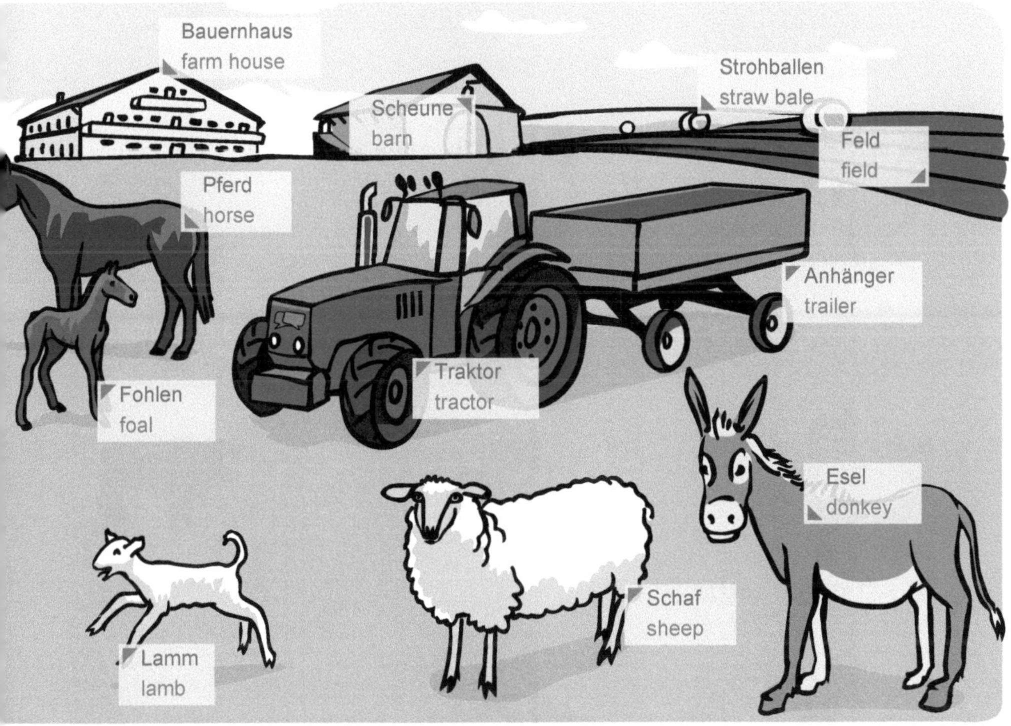

Bauernhaus
farm house
Scheune
barn
Strohballen
straw bale
Feld
field
Pferd
horse
Anhänger
trailer
Traktor
tractor
Fohlen
foal
Esel
donkey
Schaf
sheep
Lamm
lamb

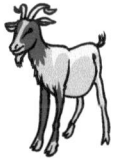

Ziege

goat

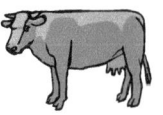

Kuh

cow

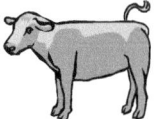

Kalb

calf

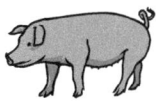

Schwein

pig

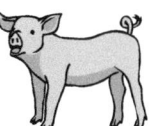

Ferkel

piglet

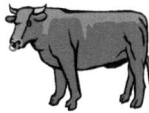

Stier

bull

Gans

goose

Ente

duck

Küken

chick

Huhn

hen

Hahn

cockerel

Ratte

rat

Katze

cat

Maus

mouse

Ochse

ox

Hund

dog

Hundehütte

dog house

Gartenschlauch

garden hose

Gießkanne

watering can

Sense

scythe

Pflug

plow

Bauernhof - farm

Sichel

sickle

Hacke

hoe

Mistgabel

pitchfork

Axt

axe

Schubkarre

pushcart

Trog

trough

Milchkanne

milk can

Sack

sack

Zaun

fence

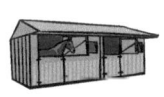

Stall

stable

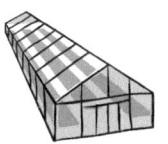

Treibhaus

greenhouse

Boden

soil

Saat

seed

Dünger

fertilizer

Mähdrescher

combine harvester

ernten
harvest

Ernte
harvest

Yamswurzel
yams

Weizen
wheat

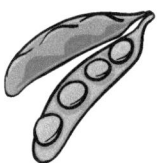

Soja
soya

Erdapfel
potato

Mais
corn

Raps
rapeseed

Obstbaum
fruit tree

Maniok
manioc

Getreide
grain

Haus

house

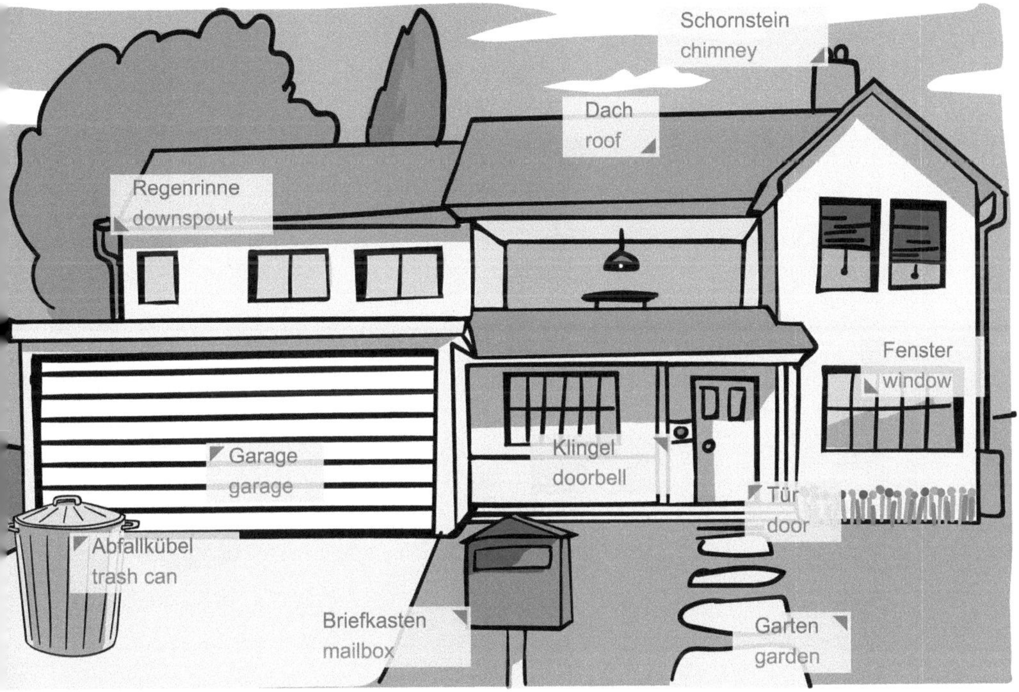

Schornstein
chimney
Dach
roof
Regenrinne
downspout
Fenster
window
Klingel
doorbell
Garage
garage
Tür
door
Abfallkübel
trash can
Briefkasten
mailbox
Garten
garden

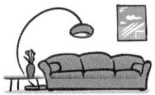

Wohnzimmer

living room

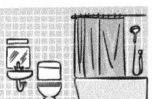

Badezimmer

bathroom

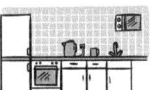

Küche

kitchen

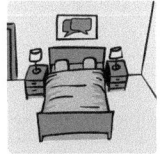

Schlafzimmer

bedroom

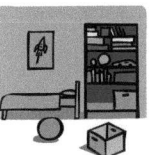

Kinderzimmer

kids room

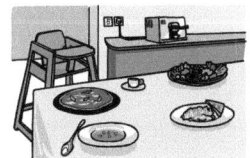

Esszimmer

dining room

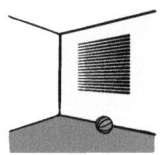

Boden

floor

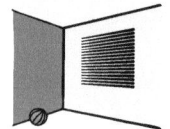

Wand

wall

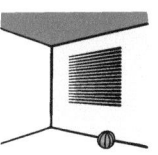

Decke

ceiling

Keller

cellar

Sauna

sauna

Balkon

balcony

Terrasse

terrace

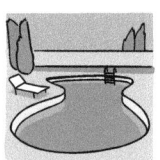

Schwimmbad

pool

Rasenmäher

lawn mower

Bettbezug

sheet

Bettdecke

bedspread

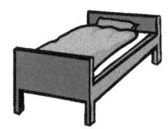

Bett

bed

Besen

broom

Kübel

bucket

Schalter

switch

Wohnzimmer
living room

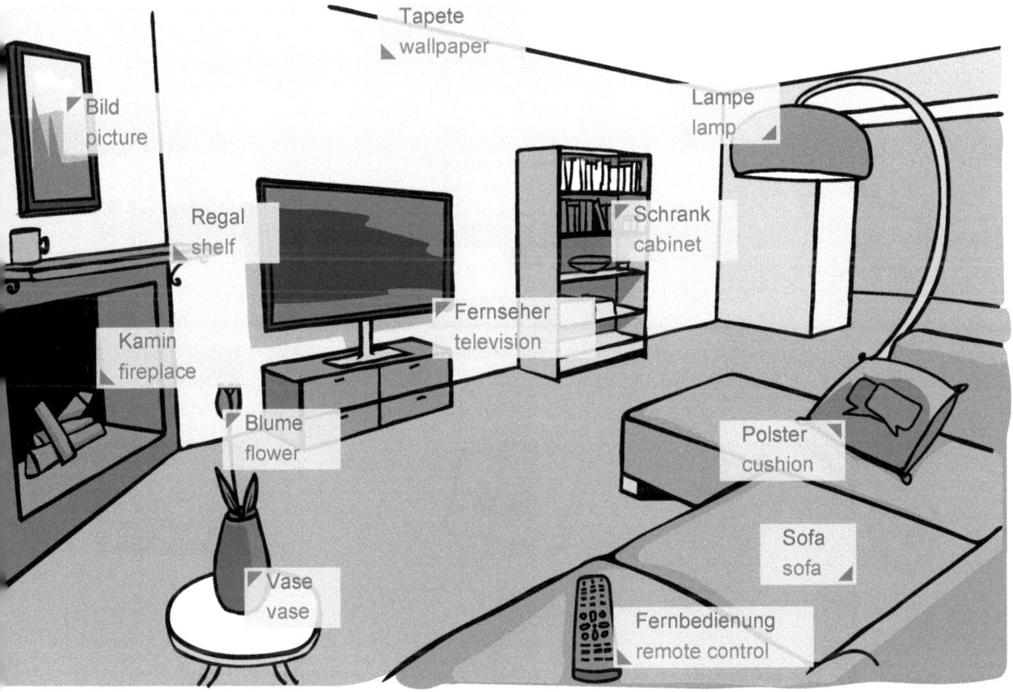
Tapete
wallpaper
Bild
picture
Lampe
lamp
Regal
shelf
Schrank
cabinet
Fernseher
television
Kamin
fireplace
Blume
flower
Polster
cushion
Sofa
sofa
Vase
vase
Fernbedienung
remote control

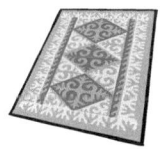

Teppich

carpet

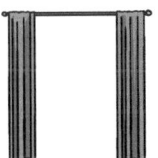

Vorhang

drape

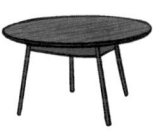

Tisch

table

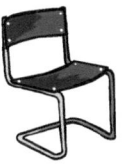

Sessel

chair

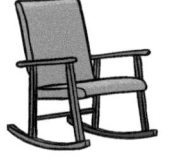

Schaukelstuhl

rocking chair

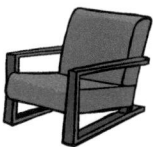

Sessel

armchair

Buch

book

Decke

blanket

Dekoration

decoration

Feuerholz

firewood

Film

film

Stereoanlage

stereo system

Schlüssel

key

Zeitung

newspaper

Gemälde

painting

Poster

poster

Radio

radio

Notizblock

notebook

Staubsauger

vacuum cleaner

Kaktus

cactus

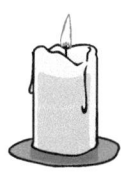

Kerze

candle

Küche
kitchen

Kühlschrank
fridge
Mikrowelle
microwave oven
Küchenwaage
kitchen scales
Toaster
toaster
Reinigungsmittel
laundry detergent
Backofen
stove
Gefrierfach
freezer
Abfallkübel
trash can
Geschirrspüler
dishwasher

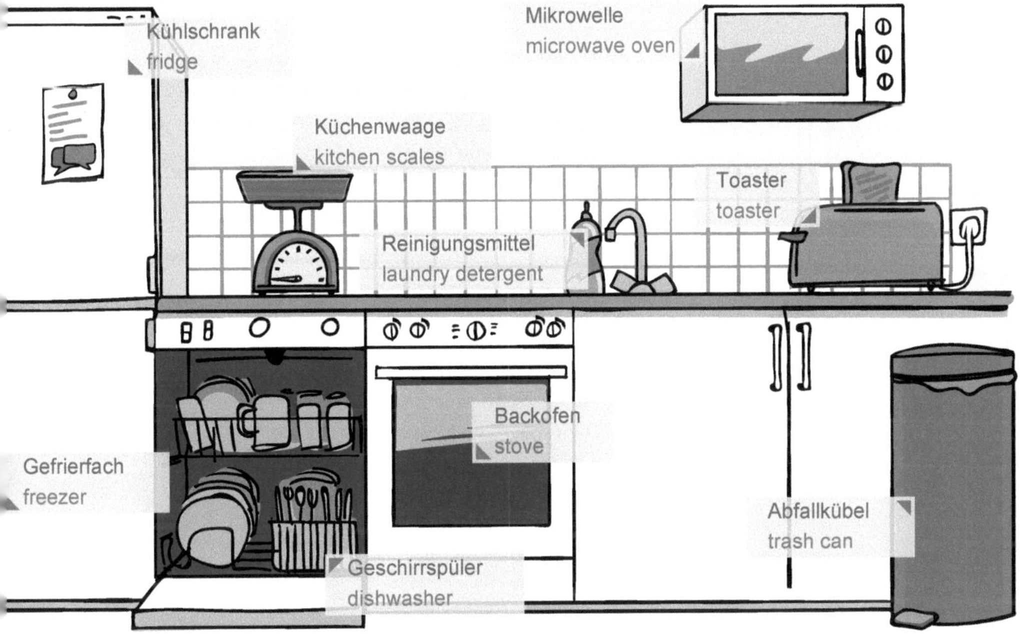

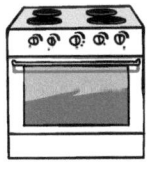

Herd

cooker

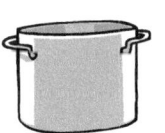

Topf

pot

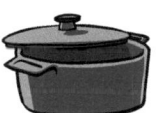

Eisentopf

cast-iron pot

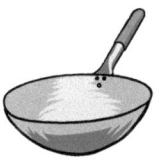

Wok / Kadai

wok / kadai

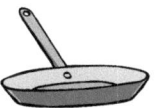

Pfanne

pan

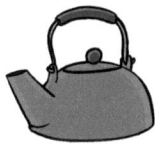

Wasserkocher

kettle

	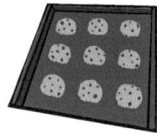	
Dampfgarer	Backblech	Geschirr
steamer	baking tray	crockery

Becher	Schale	Essstäbchen
mug	bowl	chopsticks

Schöpflöffel	Pfannenwender	Schneebesen
ladle	spatula	whisk

Kochsieb	Sieb	Reibe
strainer	sieve	grater

Mörser	Grill	Kaminfeuer
mortar	barbecue	fireplace

Schneidebrett

chopping board

Nudelholz

rolling pin

Korkenzieher

corkscrew

Dose

can

Dosenöffner

can opener

Topflappen

oven cloth

Waschbecken

sink

Bürste

brush

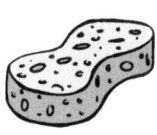

Schwamm

sponge

Mixer

blender

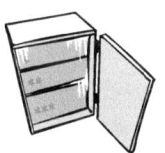

Gefriertruhe

deep freezer

Babyflasche

baby bottle

Wasserhahn

tap

Küche - kitchen

Badezimmer
bathroom

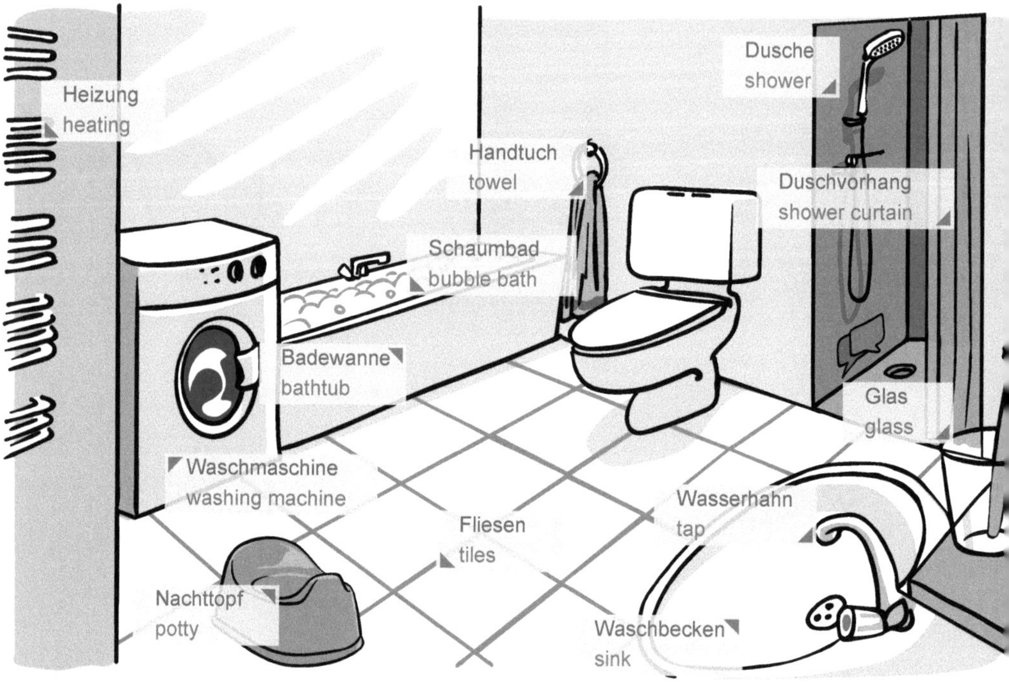

Heizung
heating
Handtuch
towel
Dusche
shower
Duschvorhang
shower curtain
Schaumbad
bubble bath
Badewanne
bathtub
Glas
glass
Waschmaschine
washing machine
Wasserhahn
tap
Fliesen
tiles
Nachttopf
potty
Waschbecken
sink

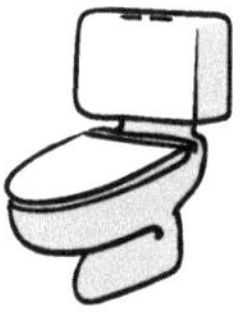

Klo

toilet

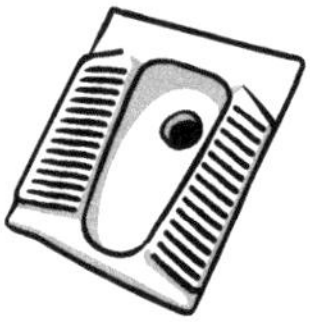

Hocktoilette

squat toilet

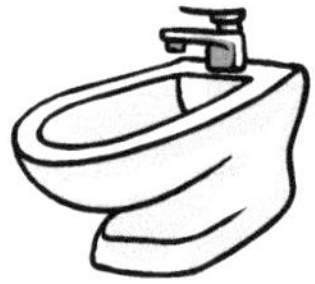

Bidet

bidet

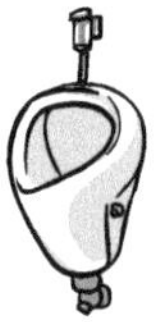

Pissoir

urinal

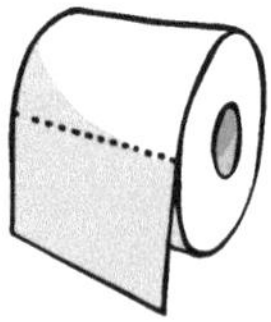

Klopapier

toilet paper

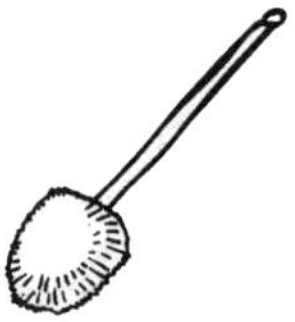

Klobürste

toilet brush

Zahnbürste

toothbrush

Zahnpasta

toothpaste

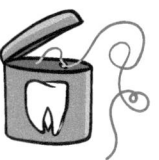

Zahnseide

dental floss

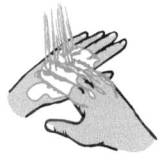

waschen

wash

Handbrause

hand shower

Intimdusche

douche

Waschschüssel

basin

Rückenbürste

back brush

Seife

soap

Duschgel

shower gel

Shampoo

shampoo

Waschlappen

flannel

Abfluss

drain

Creme

creme

Deodorant

deodorant

Spiegel

mirror

Kosmetikspiegel

hand mirror

Rasierer

razor

Rasierschaum

shaving foam

Rasierwasser

aftershave

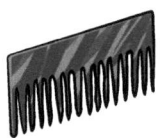

Kamm

comb

Bürste

brush

Föhn

hair-dryer

Haarspray

hairspray

Makeup

makeup

Lippenstift

lipstick

Nagellack

nail varnish

Watte

cotton wool

Nagelschere

nail scissors

Parfum

perfume

Kulturbeutel
washbag

Hocker
stool

Waage
weighing scales

Bademantel
bathrobe

Gummihandschuhe
rubber gloves

Tampon
tampon

Damenbinde
sanitary towel

Chemietoilette
chemical toilet

Kinderzimmer
kids room

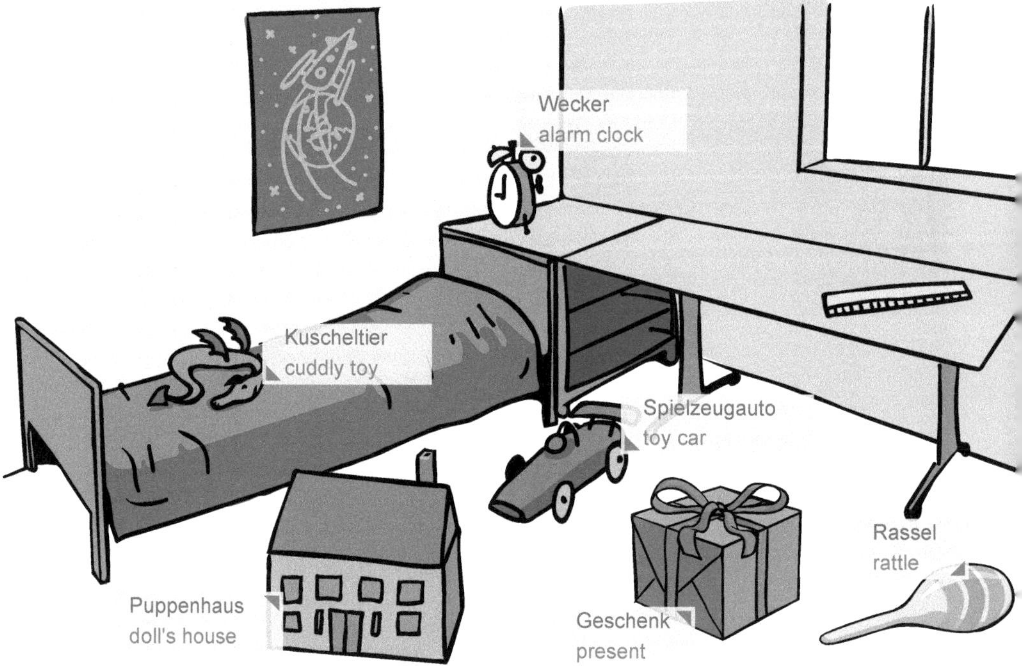
Wecker
alarm clock
Kuscheltier
cuddly toy
Spielzeugauto
toy car
Rassel
rattle
Puppenhaus
doll's house
Geschenk
present

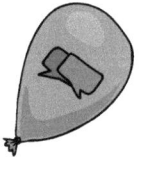

Ballon

balloon

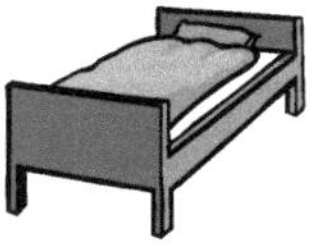

Bett

bed

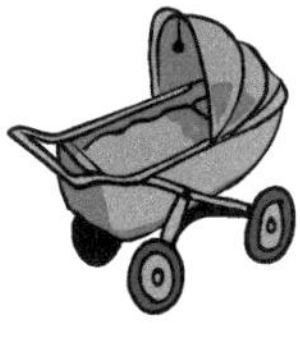

Kinderwagen

stroller

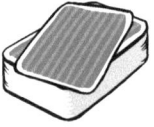

Kartenspiel

deck of cards

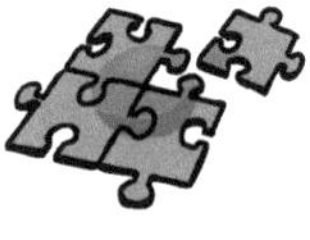

Puzzle

jigsaw

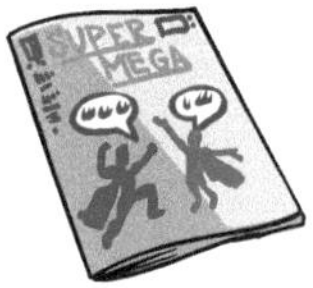
SUPER MEGA

Comic

comic

Legosteine

lego bricks

Bausteine

toy blocks

Actionfigur

action figure

Strampelanzug

romper suit

Frisbee

frisbee

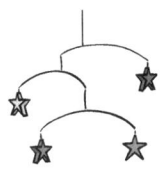

Mobile

mobile

Brettspiel

board game

Würfel

dice

Modelleisenbahn

model train set

Schnuller

pacifier

Party

party

Bilderbuch

picture book

Ball

ball

Puppe

doll

spielen

play

Sandkasten

sandpit

Schaukel

swing

Spielzeug

toys

Spielkonsole

video game console

Dreirad

tricycle

Teddy

teddy bear

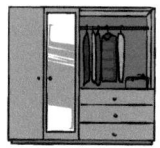

Kleiderschrank

wardrobe

Kleidung
clothing

Socken

socks

Strümpfe

stockings

Strumpfhose

tights

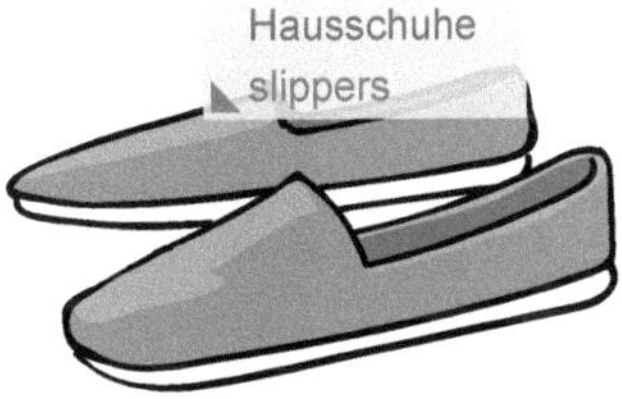

Schal
scarf

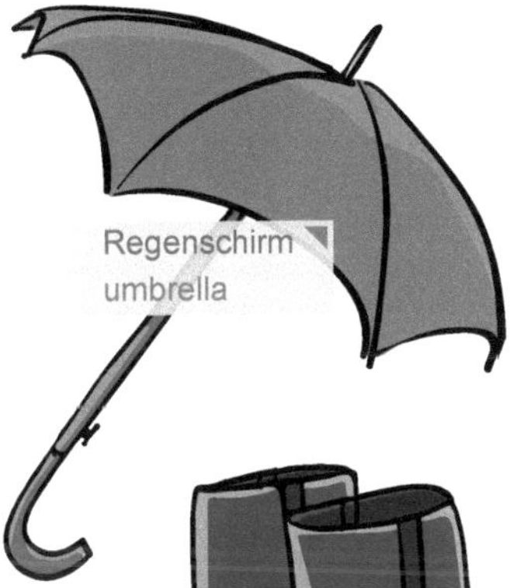

Regenschirm
umbrella

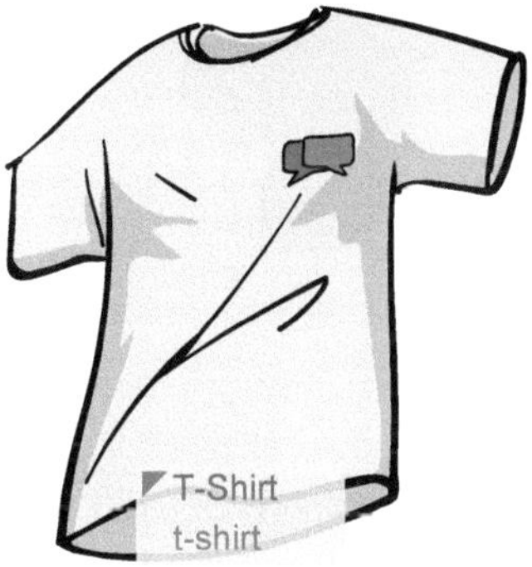

T-Shirt
t-shirt

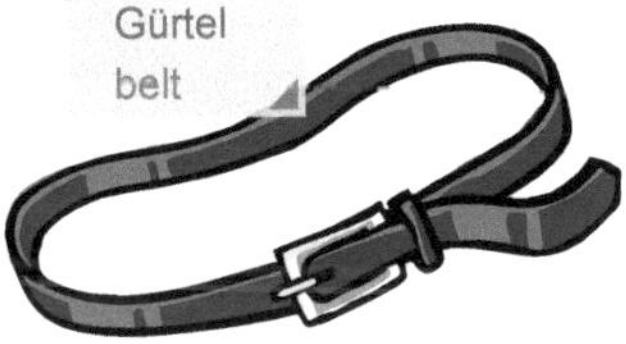

Gürtel
belt

Stiefel
boots

Hausschuhe
slippers

Turnschuhe
sneakers

Sandalen
....
sandals

Schuhe
....
shoes

Gummistiefel
....
rubber boots

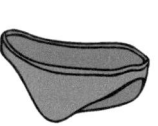

Unterhose
....
underwear

Büstenhalter
....
bra

Unterhemd
....
undershirt

Body

body

Hose

pants

Jeans

jeans

Rock

skirt

Bluse

blouse

Hemd

shirt

Pullover

pullover

Kapuzenpullover

sweater

Blazer

blazer

Jacke

jacket

Mantel

coat

Regenmantel

raincoat

Kostüm

costume

Kleid

dress

Hochzeitskleid

wedding dress

Anzug
suit

Nachthemd
nightgown

Pyjama
pajamas

Sari
sari

Kopftuch
headscarf

Turban
turban

Burka
burka

Kaftan
kaftan

Abaya
abaya

Badeanzug
swimsuit

Badehose
trunks

kurze Hose
shorts

Jogginganzug
tracksuit

Schürze
apron

Handschuhe
gloves

Knopf

button

Brille

glasses

Armband

bracelet

Halskette

necklace

Ring

ring

Ohrring

earring

Mütze

cap

Kleiderbügel

coat hanger

Hut

hat

Krawatte

tie

Reißverschluss

zip

Helm

helmet

Hosenträger

braces

Schuluniform

school uniform

Uniform

uniform

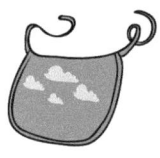

Lätzchen

bib

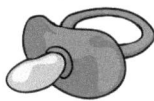

Schnuller

pacifier

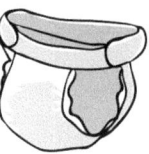

Windel

diaper

Büro
office

Server
server
Aktenschrank
filing cabinet
Drucker
printer
Papier
paper
Monitor
monitor
Maus
mouse
Schreibtisch
desk
Ordner
folder
Tastatur
keyboard
Papierkorb
waste-paper basket
Computer
computer
Sessel
chair

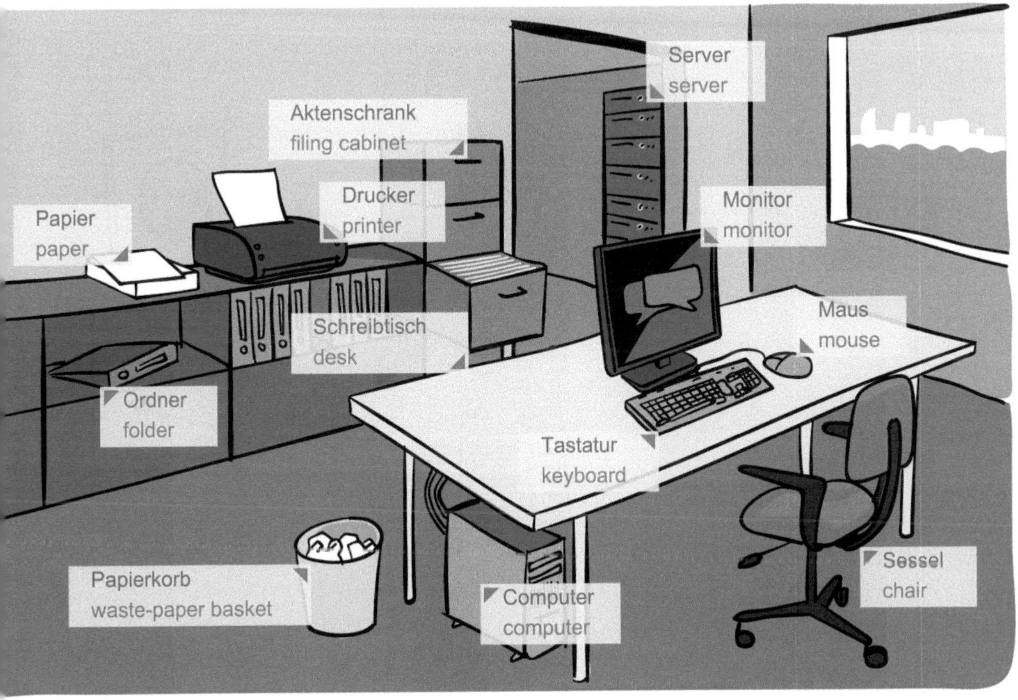

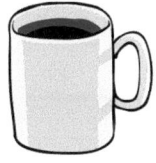

Kaffeebecher

coffee mug

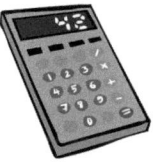

Taschenrechner

calculator

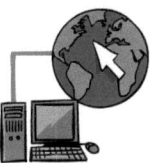

Internet

internet

Laptop
laptop

Brief
letter

Nachricht
message

Handy
cell phone

Netzwerk
network

Kopierer
photocopier

Software
software

Telefon
telephone

Steckdose
plug socket

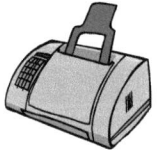

Fax
fax machine

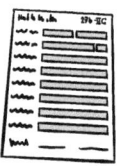

Formular
form

Dokument
document

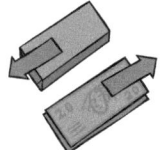

kaufen

buy

bezahlen

pay

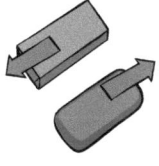

handeln

trade

Geld

money

Dollar

dollar

Euro

euro

Yen

yen

Rubel

rouble

Franken

Swiss franc

Renminbi Yuan

renminbi yuan

Rupie

rupee

Bankomat

cash point

Wechselstube

currency exchange office

Gold

gold

Silber

silver

Öl

oil

Energie

energy

Preis

price

Vertrag

contract

Steuer

tax

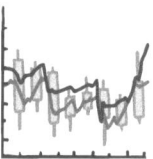

Aktie

stock

arbeiten

work

Angestellte

employee

Arbeitgeber

employer

Fabrik

factory

Geschäft

shop

Berufe

occupations

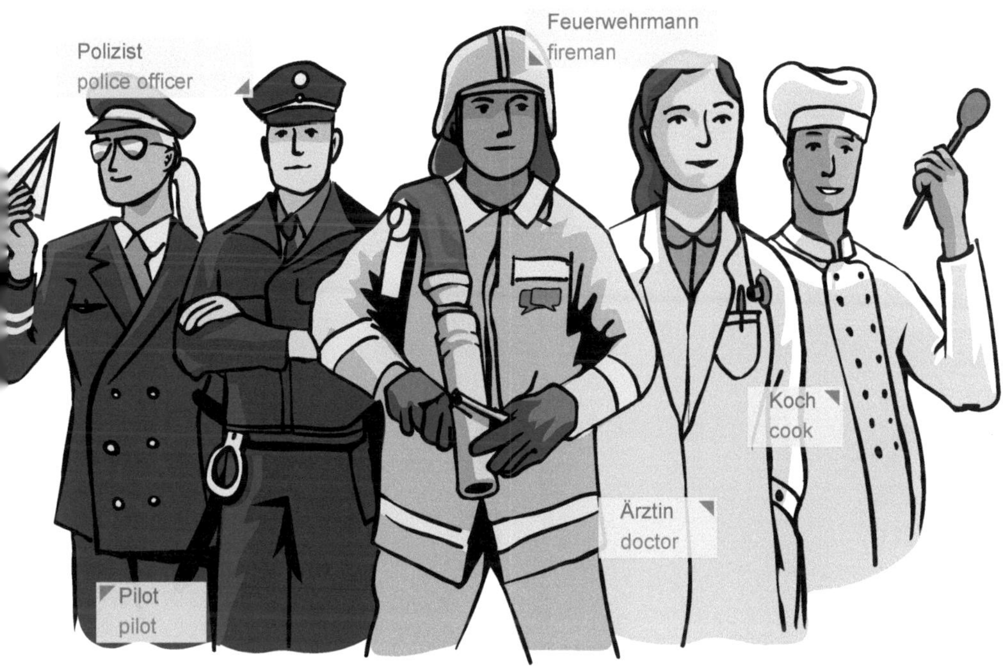

Polizist
police officer
Feuerwehrmann
fireman
Koch
cook
Ärztin
doctor
Pilot
pilot

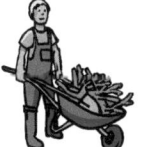

Gärtner
gardener

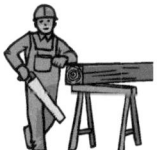

Tischler
carpenter

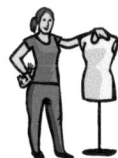

Schneiderin
seamstress

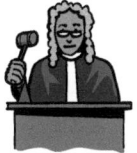

Richter
judge

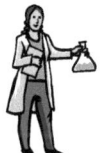

Chemikerin
chemist

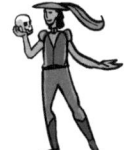

Schauspieler
actor

Busfahrer

bus driver

Taxifahrer

taxi driver

Fischer

fisherman

Putzfrau

cleaning lady

Dachdecker

roofer

Kellner

waiter

Jäger

hunter

Maler

painter

Bäcker

baker

Elektriker

electrician

Bauarbeiter

builder

Ingenieur

engineer

Schlachter

butcher

Installateur

plumber

Briefträgerin

postman

Soldat

soldier

Architekt

architect

Kassiererin

cashier

Blumenhändlerin

florist

Friseur

hairdresser

Schaffner

conductor

Mechaniker

mechanic

Kapitän

captain

Zahnärztin

dentist

Wissenschaftler

scientist

Rabbi

rabbi

Imam

imam

Mönch

monk

Pfarrer

pastor

Werkzeuge

tools

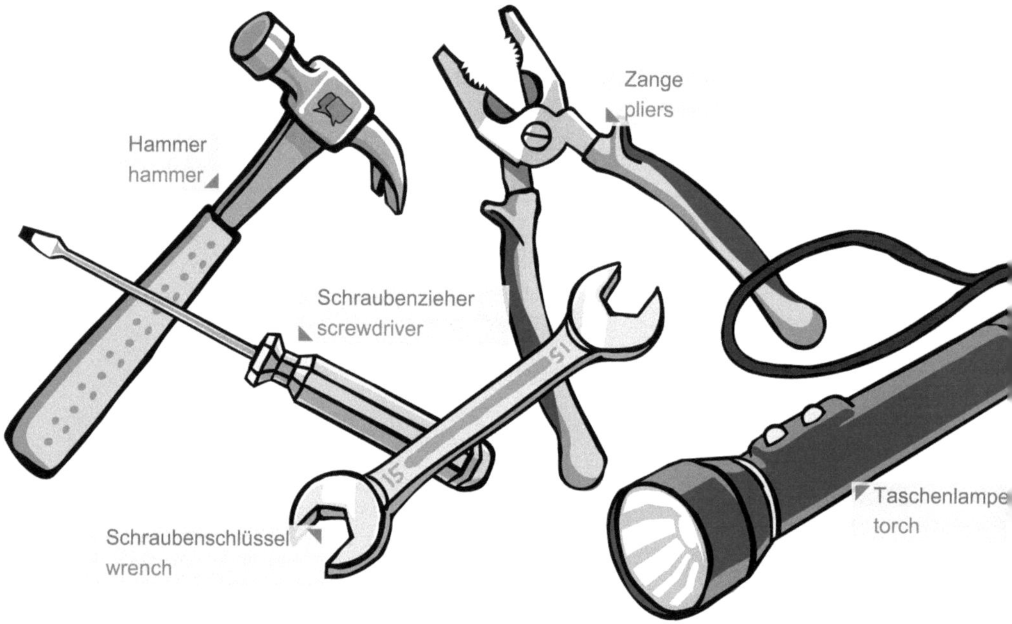
Zange
pliers
Hammer
hammer
Schraubenzieher
screwdriver
Schraubenschlüssel
wrench
Taschenlampe
torch

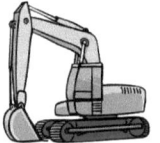

Bagger

excavator

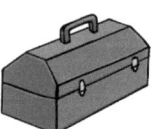

Werkzeugkasten

toolbox

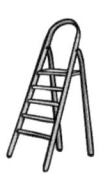

Leiter

ladder

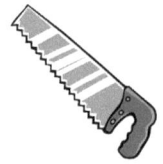

Säge

saw

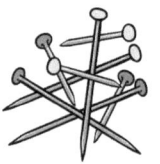

Nägel

nails

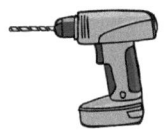

Bohrer

drill

reparieren
repair

Schaufel
shovel

Scheiße!
Damn!

Kehrschaufel
dustpan

Farbtopf
paint can

Schrauben
screws

Musikinstrumente
musical instruments

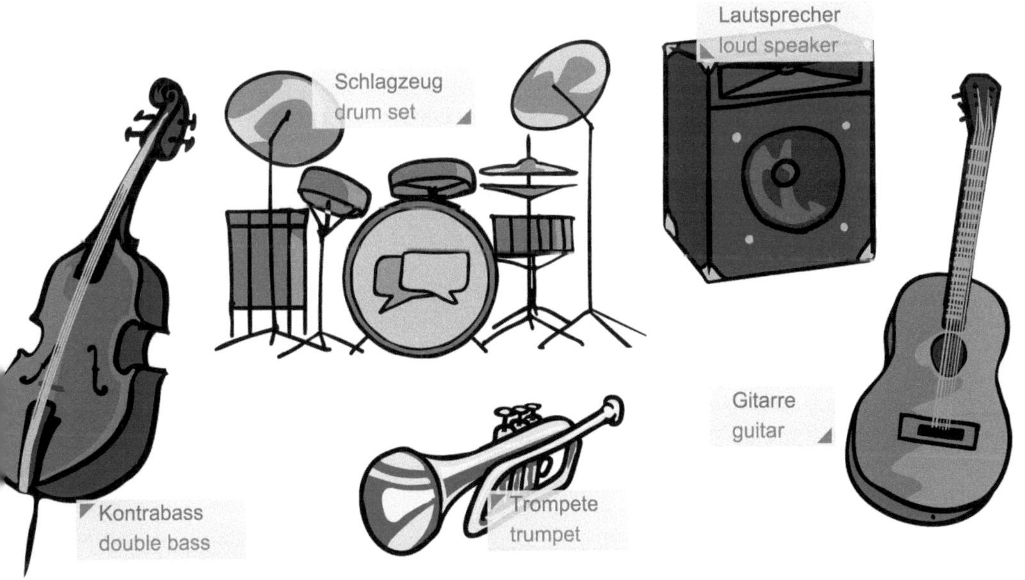

Lautsprecher
loud speaker

Schlagzeug
drum set

Gitarre
guitar

Kontrabass
double bass

Trompete
trumpet

Klavier

piano

Violine

violin

Bass

bass

Pauke

timpani

Trommeln

drums

Tastatur

keyboard

Saxophon

saxophone

Flöte

flute

Mikrofon

microphone

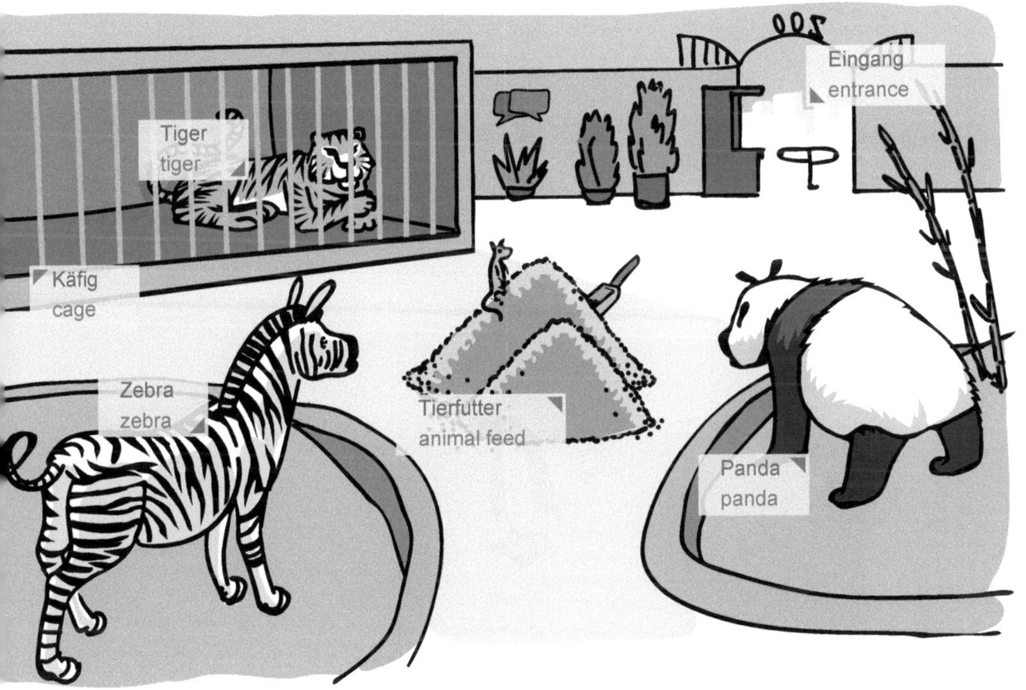

Eingang
entrance

Tiger
tiger

Käfig
cage

Zebra
zebra

Tierfutter
animal feed

Panda
panda

Tiere
animals

Elefant
elephant

Känguru
kangaroo

Nashorn
rhino

Gorilla
gorilla

Bär
bear

Kamel
camel

Strauß
ostrich

Löwe
lion

Affe
monkey

Flamingo
flamingo

Papagei
parrot

Eisbär
polar bear

Pinguin
penguin

Hai
shark

Pfau
peacock

Schlange
snake

Krokodil
crocodile

Zoowärter
zookeeper

Robbe
seal

Jaguar
jaguar

Pony

pony

Leopard

leopard

Nilpferd

hippo

Giraffe

giraffe

Adler

eagle

Wildschwein

boar

Fisch

fish

Schildkröte

turtle

Walross

walrus

Fuchs

fox

Gazelle

gazelle

American Football
American football

Radfahren
cycling

Tennis
tennis

Basketball
basketball

Schwimmen
swimming

Boxen
boxing

Eishockey
ice hockey

Fußball
soccer

Badminton
badminton

Leichtathletik
athletics

Handball
handball

Skifahren
skiing

Polo
polo

springen
jump

lachen
laugh

umarmen
hug

gehen
walk

singen
sing

träumen
dream

beten
pray

küssen
kiss

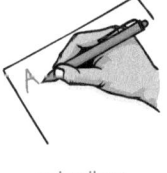

schreiben
write

zeichnen
draw

zeigen
show

drücken
push

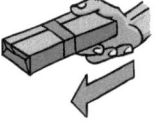

geben
give

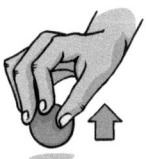

nehmen
take

haben

have

machen

do

sein

be

stehen

stand

laufen

run

ziehen

pull

werfen

throw

fallen

fall

liegen

lie

warten

wait

tragen

carry

sitzen

sit

anziehen

get dressed

schlafen

sleep

aufwachen

wake up

ansehen

look at

weinen

cry

streicheln

stroke

frisieren

comb

reden

talk

verstehen

understand

fragen

ask

hören

listen

trinken

drink

essen

eat

zusammenräumen

tidy up

lieben

love

kochen

cook

fahren

drive

fliegen

fly

Aktivitäten - activities

segeln

sail

rechnen

calculate

lesen

read

lernen

learn

arbeiten

work

heiraten

marry

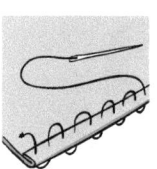

nähen

sew

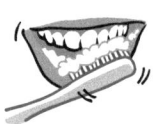

Zähne putzen

brush teeth

töten

kill

rauchen

smoke

senden

send

Familie
family

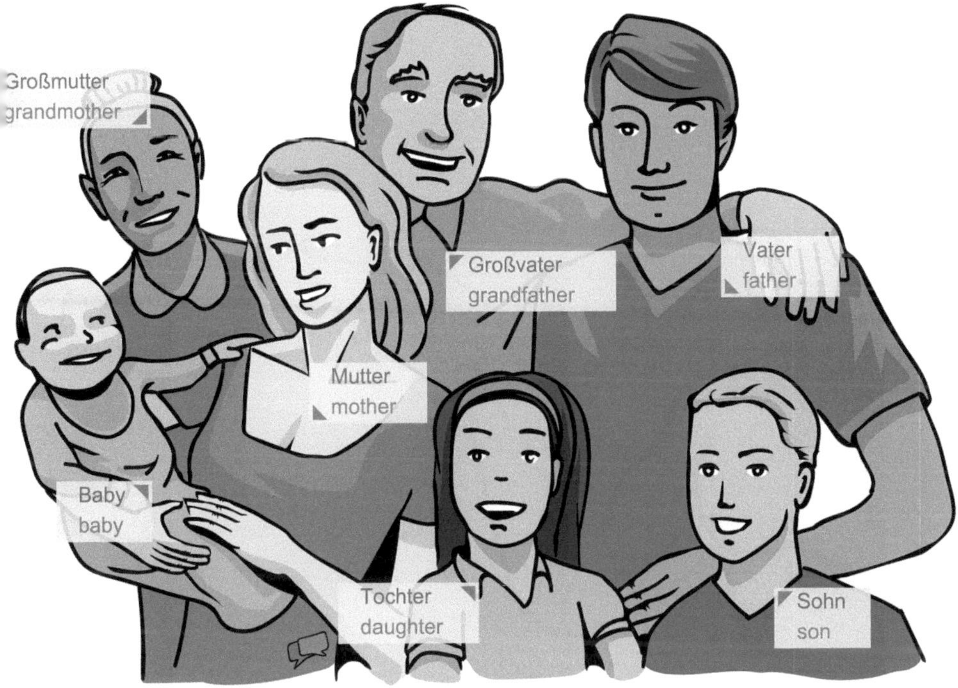

Großmutter
grandmother
Großvater
grandfather
Vater
father
Mutter
mother
Baby
baby
Tochter
daughter
Sohn
son

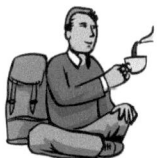

Gast

guest

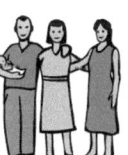

Tante

aunt

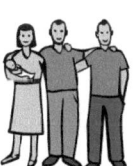

Onkel

uncle

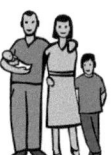

Bruder

brother

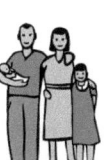

Schwester

sister

Körper

body

Stirn
forehead
Auge
eye
Schulter
shoulder
Finger
finger
Gesicht
face
Kinn
chin
Hand
hand
Bein
leg
Brust
breast
Arm
arm

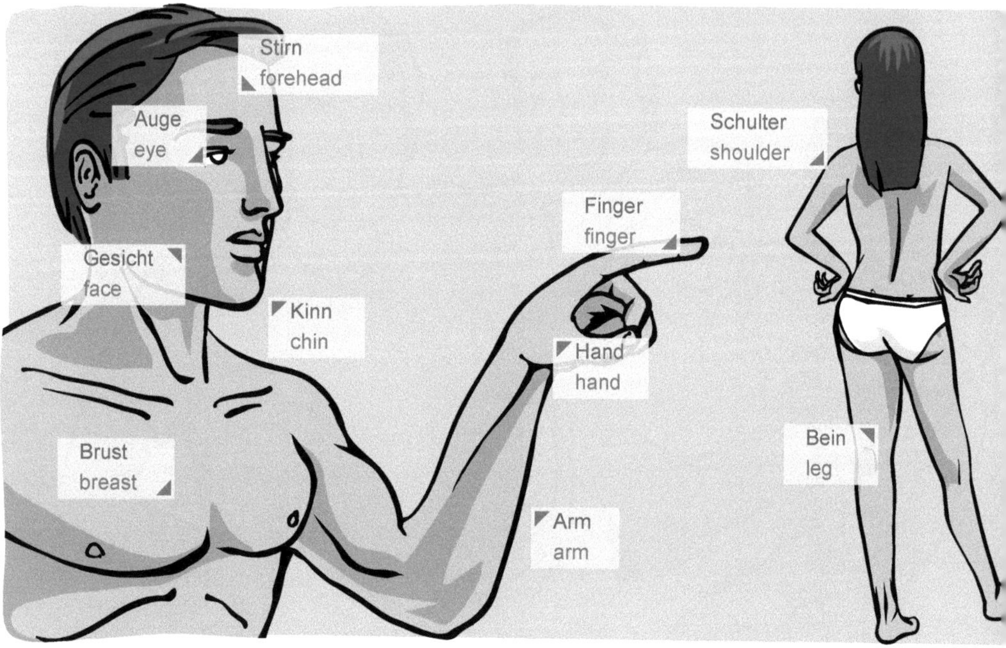

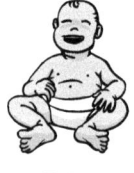

Baby

baby

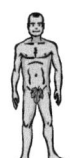

Mann

man

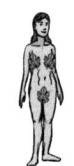

Frau

woman

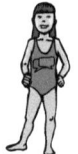

Mädchen

girl

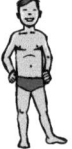

Junge

boy

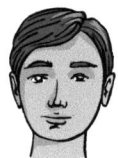

Kopf

head

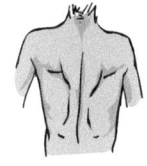

Rücken

back

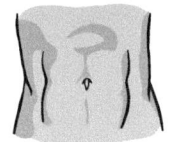

Bauch

belly

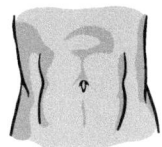

Nabel

navel

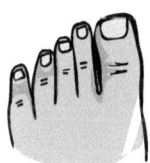

Zeh

toe

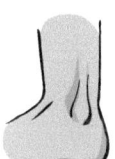

Ferse

heel

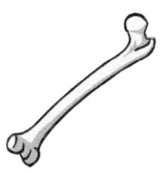

Knochen

bone

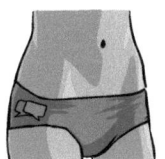

Hüfte

hip

Knie

knee

Ellbogen

elbow

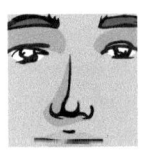

Nase

nose

Gesäß

buttocks

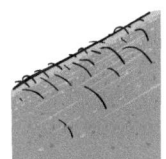

Haut

skin

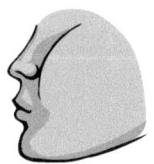

Wange

cheek

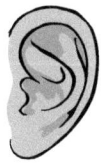

Ohr

ear

Lippe

lip

Körper - body

Mund

mouth

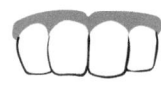

Zahn

tooth

Zunge

tongue

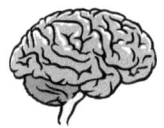

Gehirn

brain

Herz

heart

Muskel

muscle

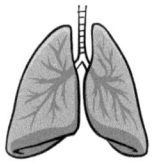

Lunge

lung

Leber

liver

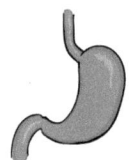

Magen

stomach

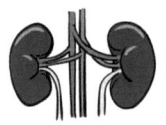

Nieren

kidneys

Geschlechtsverkehr

sex

Kondom

condom

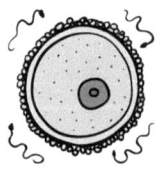

Eizelle

ovum

Sperma

semen

Schwangerschaft

pregnancy

Körper - body

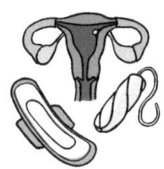

Menstruation

menstruation

Vagina

vagina

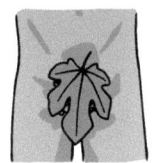

Penis

penis

Augenbraue

eyebrow

Haar

hair

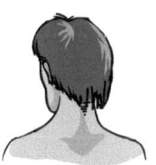

Hals

neck

Spital
hospital

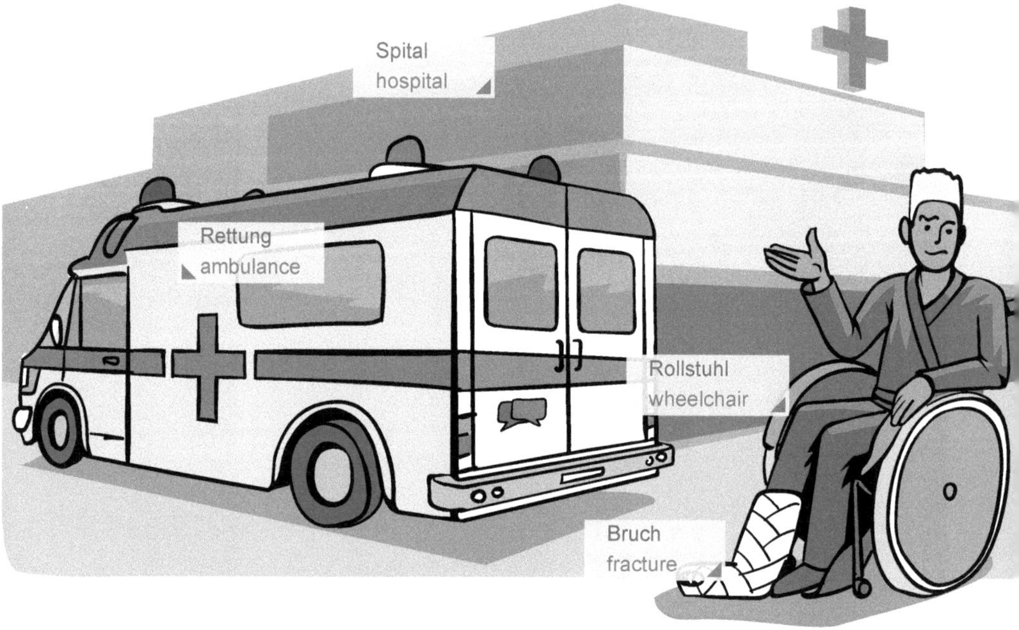

Spital
hospital
Rettung
ambulance
Rollstuhl
wheelchair
Bruch
fracture

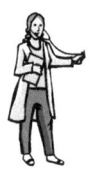

Ärztin

doctor

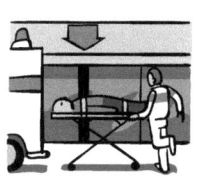

Notaufnahme

emergency room

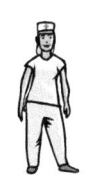

Krankenschwester

nurse

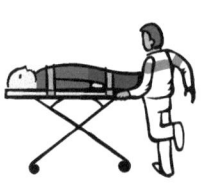

Notfall

emergency

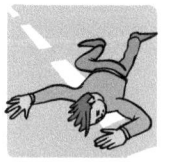

ohnmächtig

unconscious

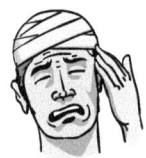

Schmerz

pain

Verletzung

injury

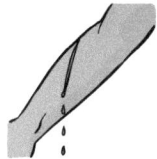

Blutung

bleeding

Herzinfarkt

heart attack

Schlaganfall

stroke

Allergie

allergy

Husten

cough

Fieber

fever

Grippe

flu

Durchfall

diarrhea

Kopfschmerzen

headache

Krebs

cancer

Diabetes

diabetes

Chirurg

surgeon

Skalpell

scalpel

Operation

operation

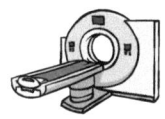

CT

CT

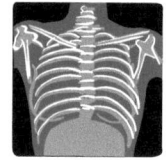

Röntgen

x-ray

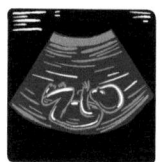

Ultraschall

ultrasound

Maske

face mask

Krankheit

disease

Wartezimmer

waiting room

Krücke

crutch

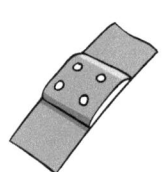

Pflaster

plaster

Verband

bandage

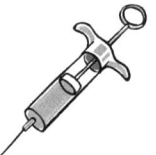

Injektion

injection

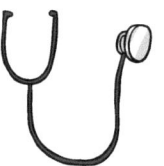

Stethoskop

stethoscope

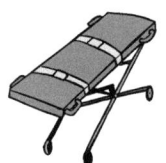

Trage

stretcher

Thermometer

clinical thermometer

Geburt

birth

Übergewicht

overweight

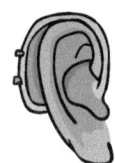

Hörgerät

hearing aid

Desinfektionsmittel

disinfectant

Infektion

infection

Virus

virus

HIV / AIDS

HIV / AIDS

Medizin

medicine

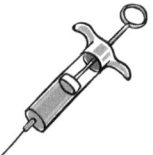

Impfung

vaccination

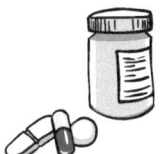

Tabletten

tablets

Pille

pill

Notruf

emergency call

Blutdruckmesser

blood pressure monitor

krank / gesund

ill / healthy

Hilfe!

Help!

Alarm

alarm

Überfall

assault

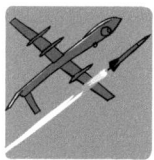

Angriff

attack

Gefahr

danger

Notausgang

emergency exit

Feuer!

Fire!

Feuerlöscher

fire extinguisher

Unfall

accident

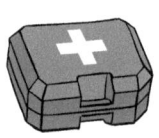

Erste-Hilfe-Koffer

first-aid kit

SOS

SOS

Polizei

police

Europa

Europe

Nordamerika

North America

Südamerika

South America

Afrika

Africa

Asien

Asia

Australien

Australia

Atlantik

Atlantic

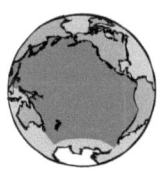

Pazifik

Pacific

Indische Ozean

Indian Ocean

Antarktische Ozean

Antarctic Ocean

Arktische Ozean

Arctic Ocean

Nordpol

North pole

Südpol

South pole

Antarktis

Antarctica

Erde

earth

Land

land

Meer

sea

Insel

island

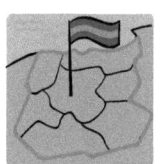

Nation

nation

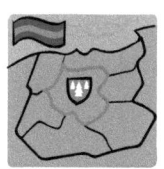

Staat

state

Ziffernblatt

clock face

Stundenzeiger

hour hand

Minutenzeiger

minute hand

Sekundenzeiger

second hand

Wie spät ist es?

What time is it?

Tag

day

Zeit

time

jetzt

now

Digitaluhr

digital watch

Minute

minute

Stunde

hour

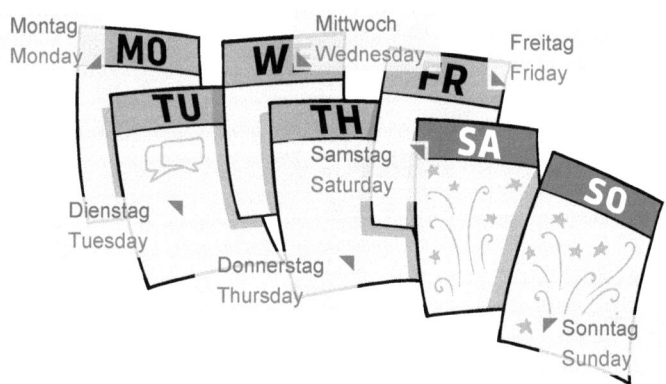

Montag / Monday
Dienstag / Tuesday
Mittwoch / Wednesday
Donnerstag / Thursday
Freitag / Friday
Samstag / Saturday
Sonntag / Sunday

gestern
yesterday

heute
today

morgen
tomorrow

Morgen
morning

Mittag
noon

Abend
evening

Arbeitstage
workdays

Wochenende
weekend

Jahr
year

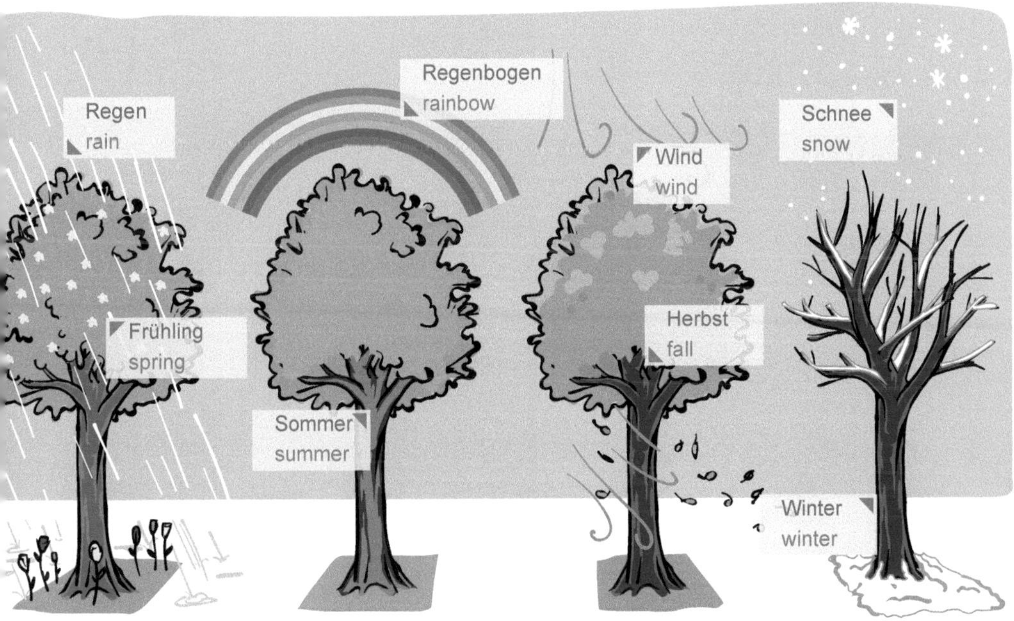
Regen
rain
Regenbogen
rainbow
Wind
wind
Schnee
snow
Frühling
spring
Herbst
fall
Sommer
summer
Winter
winter

4.APRIL 11°
5.APRIL 4°
6.APRIL 13°
7.APRIL 8°
8.APRIL 10°

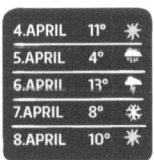

Wettervorhersage

weather forecast

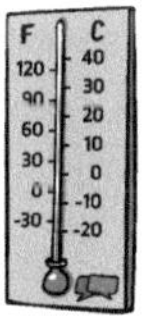
F
C
120
90
60
30
0
-30
40
30
20
10
0
-10
-20

Thermometer

thermometer

Sonnenschein

sunshine

Wolke

cloud

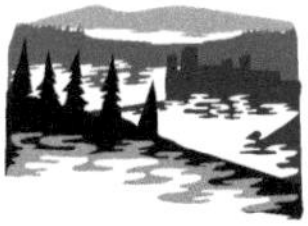

Nebel

fog

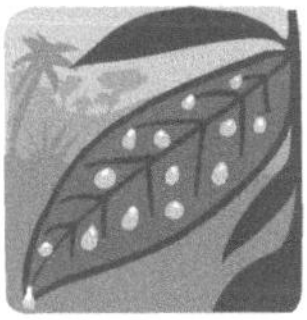

Luftfeuchtigkeit

humidity

Blitz

lightning

Donner

thunder

Sturm

storm

Hagel

hail

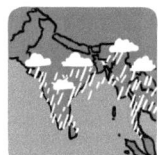

Monsun

monsoon

Flut

flood

Eis

ice

Jänner

January

Februar

February

März

March

April

April

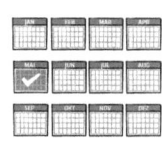

Mai

May

Juni

June

Juli

July

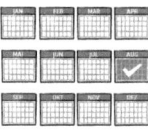

August

August

September
September

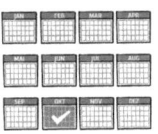

Oktober
October

November
November

Dezember
December

Formen
shapes

Kreis
circle

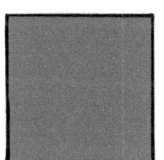

Quadrat
square

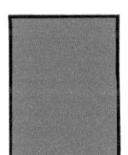

Rechteck
rectangle

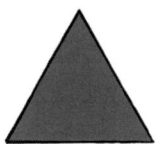

Dreieck
triangle

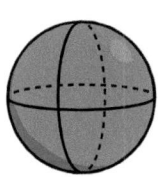

Kugel
sphere

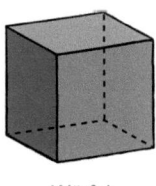

Würfel
cube

weiß

white

gelb

yellow

orange

orange

pink

pink

rot

red

lila

purple

blau

blue

grün

green

braun

brown

grau

gray

schwarz

black

viel / wenig

a lot / a little

wütend / friedlich

angry / calm

hübsch / hässlich

beautiful / ugly

Anfang / Ende

beginning / end

groß / klein

big / small

hell / dunkel

bright / dark

Bruder / Schwester

brother / sister

sauber / schmutzig

clean / dirty

vollständig / unvollständig

complete / incomplete

Tag / Nacht

day / night

tot / lebendig

dead / alive

breit / schmal

wide / narrow

genießbar / ungenießbar

edible / inedible

böse / freundlich

evil / kind

aufgeregt / gelangweilt

excited / bored

dick / dünn

fat / thin

zuerst / zuletzt

first / last

Freund / Feind

friend / enemy

voll / leer

full / empty

hart / weich

hard / soft

schwer / leicht

heavy / light

Hunger / Durst

hunger / thirst

krank / gesund

ill / healthy

illegal / legal

illegal / legal

gescheit / dumm

intelligent / stupid

links / rechts

left / right

nah / fern

near / far

neu / gebraucht

new / used

nichts / etwas

nothing / something

alt / jung

old / young

an / aus

on / off

offen / geschlossen

open / closed

leise / laut

quiet / loud

reich / arm

rich / poor

richtig / falsch

right / wrong

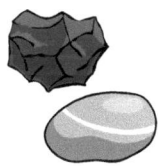

rau / glatt

rough / smooth

traurig / glücklich

sad / happy

kurz / lang

short / long

langsam / schnell

slow / fast

nass / trocken

wet / dry

warm / kühl

warm / cool

Krieg / Frieden

war / peace

0	**1**	**2**
null	eins	zwei
zero	one	two

3	**4**	**5**
drei	vier	fünf
three	four	five

6	**7**	**8**
sechs	sieben	acht
six	seven	eight

9	**10**	**11**
neun	zehn	elf
nine	ten	eleven

12

zwölf

twelve

13

dreizehn

thirteen

14

vierzehn

fourteen

15

fünfzehn

fifteen

16

sechzehn

sixteen

17

siebzehn

seventeen

18

achtzehn

eighteen

19

neunzehn

nineteen

20

zwanzig

twenty

100

hundert

hundred

1.000

tausend

thousand

1.000.000

Million

million

Englisch

English

Amerikanisches Englisch

American English

Chinesisch (Mandarin)

Chinese Mandarin

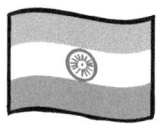

Hindi

Hindi

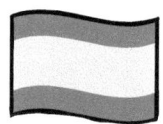

Spanisch

Spanish

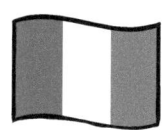

Französisch

French

Arabisch

Arabic

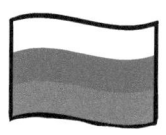

Russisch

Russian

Portugiesisch

Portuguese

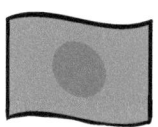

Bengalisch

Bengali

Deutsch

German

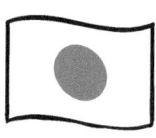

Japanisch

Japanese

ich
I

du
you

er / sie / es
he / she / it

wir
we

ihr
you

sie
they

Wer?
who?

Was?
what?

Wie?
how?

Wo?
where?

Wann?
when?

Name
name

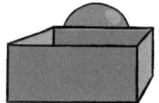

hinter

behind

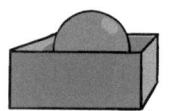

in

in

vor

in front of

über

over

auf

on

unter

under

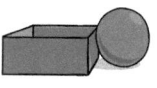

neben

beside

zwischen

between

Ort

place